PALEO BUGS

FOR KAYELLEN AND RYAN, FOR EVERYTHING

The author would like to gratefully acknowledge Dr. Alex Ross, of the London Museum of Natural History, for guiding him through selections of the Museum's amazing fossil arthropod collection.

PALEO BUGS

Survival of the Creepiest

Written and illustrated by Timothy J. Bradley

chronicle books · san francisco

A Word About the Art

Of all the creatures that have ever lived on Earth, only a very small number become fossilized. Conditions have to be just right for a creature from the ancient past to be preserved, but sometimes changes in our planet, like volcanoes and earthquakes, have damaged those fossils. Scientists sometimes have to try to imagine what an animal or plant may have looked like while it was alive from small fragments of it that became fossilized. Artists can help this process by drawing or painting pictures of what ancient life may have looked like, based on the study of fossils by paleontologists and other scientists. Since the fossilization process does not always preserve creatures completely, illustrations of extinct animals and plants will change as more fossil evidence is discovered and studied, and as new techniques are developed to study fossils.

The insects and other arthropods in this book have been illustrated with bright colors and bold patterns. Since color is not preserved through the fossilization process, we may never know what color these creatures really were. However, we can look at today's world and observe the beautiful range of pattern and color that have evolved in many arthropods over time. It's possible that some paleo bugs were as striking as the insects and their relatives we see around us now.

CONTENTS

Timeline

TO HELP ORGANIZE THE PAST, scientists divide it into chunks of time. The largest of these chunks is called an eon. Eons are broken down into eras. Eras are broken down into periods. The bugs in this book lived during three different eras: the Paleozoic era, the Mesozoic era, and the Cenozoic era.

As far as scientists know, animals first appeared on Earth during the Paleozoic era. Arthropods, including some of the creatures in this book, first appeared in Earth's oceans over 500 million years ago. The dinosaurs appeared during the Mesozoic era, which is also known as the Age of Reptiles. We are living in the most recent part of the Cenozoic era, known as the Age of Mammals.

What marks the end of an era? An extinction event is a huge catastrophe—like a meteor strike or a drastic change in Earth's climate—that wipes out large numbers of plants and animals. An extinction event occurred about 65 million years ago, marking the end of the Mesozoic era. At that time, dinosaurs (except for birds), marine reptiles, and the flying pterosaurs became extinct. The extinction event at the end of the Paleozoic era killed off almost all life on this planet.

1.   2.   3.   4.   5.   6.   7.

PALEOZOIC ERA

about 543 to 290 million years ago

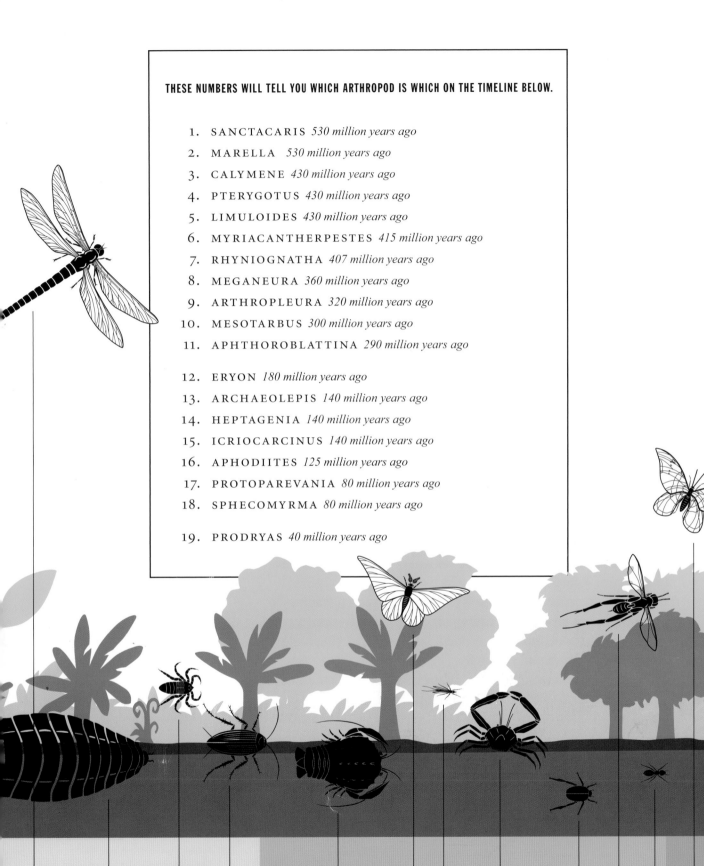

THESE NUMBERS WILL TELL YOU WHICH ARTHROPOD IS WHICH ON THE TIMELINE BELOW.

1. SANCTACARIS *530 million years ago*
2. MARELLA *530 million years ago*
3. CALYMENE *430 million years ago*
4. PTERYGOTUS *430 million years ago*
5. LIMULOIDES *430 million years ago*
6. MYRIACANTHERPESTES *415 million years ago*
7. RHYNIOGNATHA *407 million years ago*
8. MEGANEURA *360 million years ago*
9. ARTHROPLEURA *320 million years ago*
10. MESOTARBUS *300 million years ago*
11. APHTHOROBLATTINA *290 million years ago*

12. ERYON *180 million years ago*
13. ARCHAEOLEPIS *140 million years ago*
14. HEPTAGENIA *140 million years ago*
15. ICRIOCARCINUS *140 million years ago*
16. APHODIITES *125 million years ago*
17. PROTOPAREVANIA *80 million years ago*
18. SPHECOMYRMA *80 million years ago*

19. PRODRYAS *40 million years ago*

8.   9.   10.   11.   12.   13.   14.   15.   16.   17.   18.   19.

MESOZOIC ERA
about 250 to 141 million years ago

CENOZOIC ERA
about 65 million years ago to present

What Is an Arthropod?

IMAGINE: YOU TURN OVER A ROCK in your backyard, and little squirmy, crawly creatures race around trying to escape. In the flurry of jointed legs and shiny, armored bodies, you can see ants, spiders, centipedes, a daddy longlegs, and more.

Do you run screaming back into the house, or do you grab the nearest magnifying glass for a closer look? Many people are grossed out by bugs of any kind, but the truth is, insects and their relatives are amazing and necessary creatures that perform many important (and sometimes yucky!) jobs on our planet. They are extremely flexible, adapting not only to meet drastic changes on Earth but even to life in and around human cities and towns.

Scientifically speaking, insects are arthropods (ARTH-row-pods), which means "jointed leg." One look at an ant or a centipede, and you can see why. Other arthropods are related to insects, like scorpions, crabs, and lobsters.

About 570 million years ago, during the beginning of the Paleozoic era, many strange and amazing arthropods were evolving in the oceans. (Nothing lived on land yet!) Paleontologists refer to this time as the "Cambrian explosion" because new creatures appeared rapidly. Some were arthropods, but scientists are puzzled by others. Many of those ancient arthropods were unique, meaning that they are not related to present-day arthropods. Over time the creatures spread through the oceans and onto land. Some evolved wings and were the first animals on Earth to fly.

Arthropods today live in some of the most hostile conditions on our planet. Amazingly, some, like the horseshoe crab and the lowly cockroach, haven't changed much since they first developed hundreds of millions of years ago. The ability to adapt and survive in a changing environment has made insects and other arthropods some of the most successful creatures ever to live on Earth.

Scientists classify arthropods into five major groups, based on the special characteristics each group has:

MYRIAPODS *(MEER-ee-ah-pods)*
- *Includes millipedes and centipedes*
- *Bodies are divided into the head and the trunk, which is made up of lots of identical segments*
- *Each segment has the same set of organs and either one pair of legs (for centipedes) or two pairs of legs (for millipedes)*
- *Heads have one pair of antennae*

CHELICERATES *(kuh-LISS er-uts)*
- *Includes spiders, mites, and scorpions*
- *Bodies are divided into two parts: the head—or cephalothorax (seff-a-low-THOR-ax)—and the abdomen*
- *Heads have no antennae, but have two sets of limbs called chelicerae (kuh-LISS-er-ee) and pedipalps (PED-ih-palps) used for sensing the environment or catching food*

CRUSTACEANS *(crus-TAY-shuns)*
- *Includes crabs, lobsters, shrimp, and isopods (EYE-so-pods), like pill bugs*
- *Bodies are divided into two parts: the cephalothorax and the abdomen*
- *Heads have two pairs of antennae, and three pairs of limbs around their mouths*

INSECTS
- *Includes beetles, ants, bees, and wasps*
- *Bodies are divided into three parts: head, thorax, and abdomen*
- *Heads have one pair of antennae*
- *Thoraxes have three pairs of limbs and usually one or two pairs of wings*

TRILOBITES *(TRY-low-bites)*
- *Extinct, crawled and swam through the Paleozoic oceans for 300 million years*
- *Bodies had three parts: the cephalon (SEFF-uh-lon), or head; the thorax; and the pygidium (pie-JID-ee-um), or tail*
- *Bodies also divided into three parts along their length (trilobite means "three lobes")*
- *One pair of antennae on their heads*
- *Many pairs of walking limbs with gills on their thoraxes*

The Characteristics of Arthropods

Arthropods, both extinct and living, have a few things in common:

Arthropods are bilaterally symmetrical, which means that the left side of their body is the mirror image of the right side.

Arthropods are invertebrates (in-VERT-uh-brits), which means they do not have backbones. Their hard exoskeleton provides a frame to which their muscles are attached.

Arthropods' bodies are divided into segments. The segments often contain identical sets of internal organs. Insects have three body sections, while spiders have two.

Arthropods have an exoskeleton (ex-oh-SKELL-uh-tin), a hard shell, or casing, on the outside of their bodies that provides structure and protection. This is very different from mammals, reptiles, amphibians, and fish, which have skeletons inside their bodies. To grow, an arthropod must molt, or shed, its exoskeleton and replace it with a larger one.

Arthropods have flexible, jointed legs. Muscles attached to either side of the joint make the leg move.

Arthropods have many pairs of limbs. In some arthropods like spiders, crabs, and insects, some of these limbs have evolved into special tools for eating, grasping, and sensing the environment. Different arthropods have different numbers of limbs; insects have six limbs for movement, while spiders have eight.

Paleozoic Arthropods and Their Relatives
—The Shape of Things to Come

IMAGINE: ABOUT 530 MILLION years ago, in an area of Earth we now call Canada, a very strange creature is poking along the sea floor next to a steep underwater wall. The creature has five domed eyes, a nozzle reaching out from underneath the front of its body with spiny jaws at the end, and a body covered with plates. This is *Opabinia*, a bizarre 2½-inch-long creature that swam in the seas during the Cambrian period. It is looking for tiny crawling things that live on the sandy sea bottom. Predatory worms, called *Ottoia*, poke their toothy mouths out of the sand as *Opabinia* paddles around the sponges growing on the bottom. It comes across an abandoned bit of trilobite shell and then another. A very young trilobite has molted; while its new exoskeleton is still soft, it will be easy prey.

Suddenly, spiny legs grab unsuspecting *Opabinia*. *Sanctacaris*, a 4-inch-long swimming arthropod—another hunter in these Cambrian seas—has just caught its lunch. *Sanctacaris* waves its paddle-shaped limbs softly to hold its position. *Sanctacaris* has a large head shield, overlapping armor plates along its back, and a tail that looks something like that of a lobster. *Sanctacaris* is considered an early member of the chelicerate (kuh-LISS-er-ut) group of arthropods, which includes our modern-day spiders and scorpions. *Sanctacaris'* spiny grasping arms feed the struggling *Opabinia* into its mouth. It starts to crunch away at *Opabinia*'s hard outer skeleton and, within a few short minutes, *Sanctacaris* is ready to start searching for its next meal.

Just then, strong vibrations shoot through the water. An undersea hillside collapses and blocks out the light from the surface. A wall of sediment swiftly rains down and buries *Sanctacaris* and the other creatures living here on the sea floor under a thick layer of mud.

Hundreds of millions of years later, scientists discover the fossils of the creatures buried under that ancient mudslide. After some study they recognize some of the creatures as true arthropods, but many do not fit neatly into any arthropod group. Scientists decide they may have been evolutionary "experiments" that didn't survive past the Cambrian period.

THE ARTHROPODS OF THE PALEOZOIC ERA INCLUDE: *Sanctacaris* (a chelicerate), *Marella* (a unique arthropod), *Calymene* (a trilobite), *Pterygotus* (a sea scorpion), *Limuloides* (an ancient horseshoe crab), *Myriacantherpestes* (a spiky millipede), *Rhyniognatha* (an early insect), *Meganeura* (a giant dragonfly), *Arthropleura* (a huge armored millipede), and *Aphthoroblattina* (an ancient cockroach).

SANCTACARIS

(SANK-TAH-CARE-ISS) • *530 million years ago*

SANCTACARIS, A 4-INCH-LONG armored arthropod, first appeared about 30 million years into the Paleozoic era. Scientists believe that *Sanctacaris* was an ancient chelicerate related to the spiders and scorpions we see today. It had six pairs of limbs on its wide head, which is a characteristic of chelicerates. Along its sides, it had a row of paddle-shaped limbs that also held gills for breathing. These double-sectioned limbs are biramous (BYE-ram-us), meaning they have two parts. On its last segment,

Sanctacaris had a wide, flat tail, called a telson, which would have helped it move quickly through the water in search of prey.

Sanctacaris was probably an efficient predator of the Cambrian seas, but it had to avoid an even bigger carnivore: the huge *Anomalocaris*, which reached 2 feet in length.

MARELLA

(MAH-RELL-UH) · *530 million years ago*

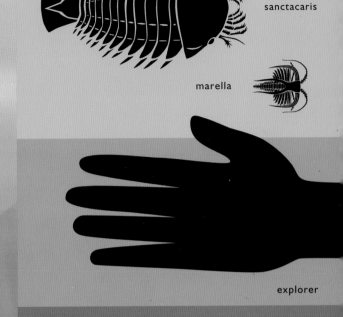

sanctacaris

marella

explorer

MARELLA LIVED AT THE SAME TIME AS *Sanctacaris*. It was less than an inch long, and had a large head shield with four large spines curving gracefully back over its body. Scientists believe that *Marella* crawled along the ocean bottom, feeling about for any particles of food with its antennae. Fossils of *Marella* show that its body contained from 24 to 26 segments. Each segment had a pair of biramous limbs. The lower section was for walking, and the upper section featured feathery gills for breathing. The last body segment, the telson, was very small. While *Marella* is considered an arthropod, it may not be directly related to the kind of arthropods living today.

STRANGE CREATURES FROM THE BURGESS SHALE

The fossil formation where Sanctacaris *and* Marella *were found is called the Burgess Shale, located in Yoho National Park in Canada. About 530 million years ago, an underwater mudslide buried many strange creatures here, amazingly preserving many of the soft body parts that do not usually become fossilized. It is possible that the mudslide swept the creatures into a lower underwater trench where the lack of oxygen in the water kept the creatures from decomposing. Fossils from the Burgess Shale were originally found in the early 1900s, but were reexamined in the 1970s with modern techniques and instruments, with baffling results. After extensive research, paleontologists feel that some of the creatures found here, like* Opabinia, Nectocaris, *and* Anomalocaris, *might have been unique, meaning they do not have any surviving relatives beyond the Cambrian period. These creatures show that there is much still to learn about the life of the distant past.*

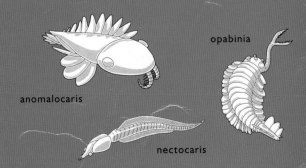

anomalocaris

opabinia

nectocaris

CALYMENE

(CAL-EE-MEEN) • *430 million years ago*

Like all arthropods, trilobites were divided into many segments. But unlike most arthropods, trilobites were also divided lengthwise into three sections, or lobes. The two outer lobes are called pleura (PLOOR-ah), and the center lobe is called the axis.

Typically, only a trilobite's hard outer shell is preserved as a fossil because the rest of its body was too soft to survive. But scientists have found trilobite fossils that show their legs were biramous, with both walking and gill sections. Trilobites also had antennae to help them sense the world around them.

Calymene was a small 4-inch-long trilobite predator that crawled across the sea bottom during the Silurian (sih-LURE-ee-an) period. It had small eyes on its cephalon. Its body, or thorax, was made up of 13 segments, and its small tail, or pygidium, made up of 7 segments fused, or stuck, together.

In some fossils, *Calymene* is rolled up in a ball, much like a modern-day pill-bug when threatened. This may have been how *Calymene* defended itself from attack.

PTERYGOTUS

(TERR-EE-GOAT-US) • *430 million years ago*

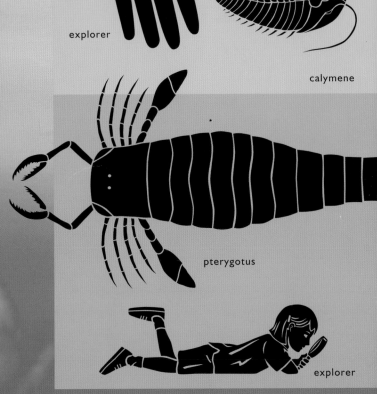

explorer

calymene

pterygotus

explorer

PTERYGOTUS WAS A FEROCIOUS 9-foot-long ocean creature that belonged to a group of arthropods called eurypterids (yoo-RIP-ter-ids) or "sea scorpions." *Pterygotus* looked a little like a flattened modern-day scorpion, but it had some amazing adaptations that allowed it to live in the ocean. One set of its forward limbs had grabbing claws, which would have helped it catch its prey. Its flat body shape and paddle-shaped limbs may have helped it maneuver in the water. During the Silurian period, sea scorpions like *Pterygotus* were probably the top predators in the oceans.

RADIASPIS, A SUPER-SPINY TRILOBITE

Some trilobites had an amazing array of spines sticking out of their bodies. Fossils of these creatures have been discovered in the part of the world we now call Morocco. Radiaspis (ray-dee-AS-pis) is one of these super-spiny trilobites. A pair of spines grew from its head shield, and several more grew from the back of its head and arched over its thorax. Another pair of long spines grew from each segment of Radiaspis' thorax, and a series of spines grew from its tail. These spines may have protected Radiaspis from predators. Judging by the size of the spines, Radiaspis must have lived in a very dangerous neighborhood!

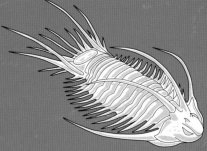

LIMULOIDES

(LIM-yoo-LOYD-eez) • *430 million years ago*

Limuloides was an ancient arthropod related to today's horseshoe crab. In many ways, it looked very similar to the horseshoe crab, but *Limuloides* was able to roll its armored body into a ball, like *Calymene*, possibly for defense. That's something a modern horseshoe crab can't do. *Limuloides* had compound eyes that helped it sense its environment. Scientists believe that *Limuloides* lived in saltwater lagoons or areas where a river emptied into the ocean. Relatives of *Limuloides* evolved to live in fresh water like lakes or rivers.

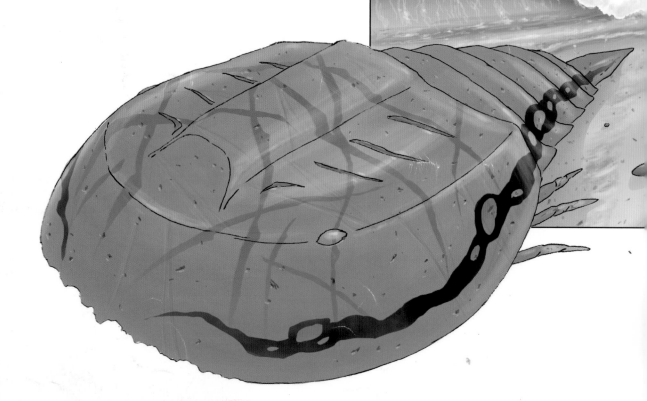

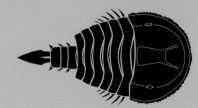

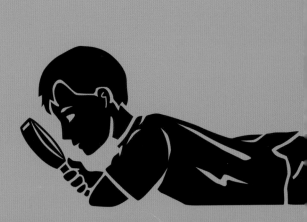

explorer

MODERN-DAY
HORSESHOE CRABS

The horseshoe crab Limulus *(LIM-yoo-luss)
can be found in today's oceans, and if you were
able to place it next to the ancient* Limuloides,
*you would see that horseshoe crabs have not
changed much in over 400 million years.*

*Horseshoe crabs are not really crabs.
They are chelicerate arthropods, more closely
related to spiders and scorpions. Horseshoe
crabs forage on the sea floor for worms and
mollusks. Underneath their carapace, or shell,
they have pincers for grasping and cutting up
prey. Gills allow them to get oxygen from the
water, but horseshoe crabs can survive on land
for a short time.*

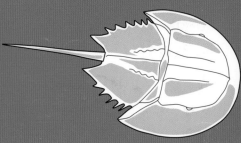

MYRIACANTHERPESTES

(MEER-E-UH-CAN-THER-PEST-EEZ) • *415 million years ago*

Myriacantherpestes, which lived in the middle of the Silurian period, is believed to be one of the first arthropods ever to live on land. It belongs to a group of arthropods called *myriapods*, which means "thousand legs." Modern-day centipedes and millipedes are myriapods, and if you've ever seen one, you will understand why. *Myriacantherpestes* had many armored and spiked body segments, which may have been a defense from predators, or a way to identify each other.

RHYNIOGNATHA

(RY-NEE-OH-NAY-THAH) • *407 million years ago*

According to the fossil record, the oldest insect currently known is called *Rhyniognatha*, discovered in a fossil-filled area called the Rhynie Chert in Aberdeen, Scotland. Although the entire insect wasn't preserved, paleontologists believe that *Rhyniognatha*'s head and scissorlike jaws were similar to those of modern flying insects. Although *Rhyniognatha* lived over 400 million years ago, it may have looked similar to today's mayfly.

explorer

rhyniognatha

myriacantherpestes

explorer

WINGS FOR SURVIVAL

Insects were the first creatures on Earth to fly, giving them a very effective way to locate and catch their food and escape enemies.

Wings might have appeared as a way to help insects warm their bodies so they could move quickly. When the air is cool, insects become sluggish. Big wings increase the surface area of the insect, and soak up more heat from the sun. If an insect could warm its body more quickly than its prey, it would have the energy to hunt efficiently and effectively.

Wings can also be used for protection. In some insects, like beetles, wings evolved into hard shells called elytra *(ee-LIE-trah). These tough shells protect a beetle's second pair of wings when it is not flying.*

Other insects, like butterflies and moths, have markings on their wings that look like eyes. When threatened, they open their wings, revealing what looks like the eyes of a predator.

21

MEGANEURA

(MEG-AH-NUR-uh) • *360 million years ago*

MEGANEURA WAS A HUGE DRAGONFLY with a 3-foot wingspan that lived during the Carboniferous (kar-bun-IFF-ur-us) period. If you spread your arms out as wide as you can, you will see how big *Meganeura*'s wings were. Except for its giant size, it probably looked very similar to the dragonflies we can see flitting over streams and lakes today. Because of its great size and delicate wings, *Meganeura* probably preferred to hunt smaller insects (including other dragonflies) and maybe even small reptiles and fish in open areas like streams and lakes. If its wings were damaged, this huge insect would be stuck on the ground and vulnerable to predators.

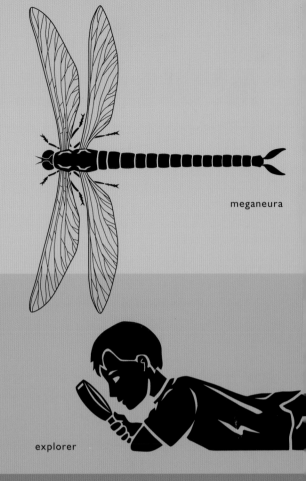

meganeura

explorer

DRAGONFLY LIFE CYCLE

Dragonflies go through several growth stages
before they become adults. After
hatching from eggs, they
spend time living
underwater as nymphs,
which are very different from
adult dragonflies. Dragonfly nymphs
are ferocious predators and will eat
almost any creature they can catch. Their
hinged lower jaw extends so they can snag their
prey with their sharp fangs. If Meganeura went
through a similar growth stage as it grew toward
adulthood, it was probably a voracious underwater
killer. Dragonfly nymphs know instinctively when
it is time to crawl out of the water for the last time
and emerge as an adult dragonfly. Once its exoskel-
eton hardens and dries, the dragonfly is ready for
its life on the wing.

ARTHROPLEURA

(ARTH-row-PLOOR-ah) • *320 million years ago*

ARTHROPLEURA WAS A GIANT MEMBER of the myriapod group of arthropods. Fossils indicate that this extinct millipede could reach lengths of 7 feet! *Arthropleura* was an herbivore equipped with a heavily armored exoskeleton on its segmented body. The armor plates curved over each body segment and then continued over its sides, form- ing a protective shield that fanned out over its legs. *Arthropleura*'s armor had a knobby texture. Fossils of *Arthropleura*'s exoskeleton and the trackways it made with its many legs as it walked through mud have been found in rocks from the middle Carbon- iferous period.

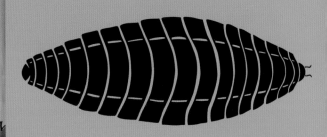

arthropleura

explorer

GIANT AFRICAN MILLIPEDE

This present-day myriapod, with species living in Africa, can reach lengths of up to $8^{1}/_{2}$ inches. Giant African millipedes eat leaves. They aren't heavily armored, like Arthropleura *was, but when threatened, they can secrete an acidic liquid that causes irritation to predators. However, millipedes are very docile, and many people keep these big arthropods as pets.*

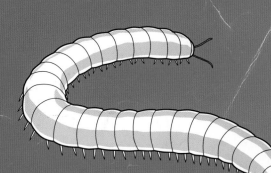

MESOTARBUS

(MEE-so-TAR-bus) • *300 million years ago*

Even though Mesotarbus was a very tiny creature—about three-quarters of an inch long—it must have been ferocious. Scientists classify *Mesotarbus* in a group of arthropods called phalangiotarbids (fay-LANJ-ee-oh-TAR-bids), which were ancient spider relatives. Because *Mesotarbus* lacks the spinnerets that spiders use to make silk, paleontologists believe that it was an ambush predator, waiting patiently for prey to come near enough to attack. Fossils don't reveal everything about *Mesotarbus'* mouthparts, but looking at the sturdy legs and claws, it is easy to imagine this tiny hunter preying on insects that came too close.

mesotarbus

explorer

THE BIGGEST SPIDER? NOPE!

Paleontologists were astonished when they uncovered a fossil of what they thought was the biggest spider that ever lived. The fossil was given the name Megarachne *(meg-uh-RACK-nee), and scientists believed that the spider was about as big as an adult person's head and that it may have had a 20-inch leg span. It was a very exciting discovery!*

Recently, Megarachne *fossils have been re-examined, and paleontologists now believe they were probably eurypterids, or sea scorpions.*

As scientists and paleontologists develop more effective tools and instruments to uncover and examine fossils, our understanding of the distant past will undoubtedly evolve.

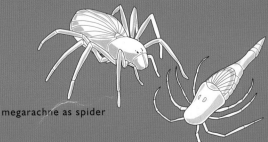

megarachne as spider

megarachne as sea scorpion

APHTHOROBLATTINA

(AFF-THOR-OH-BLAT-EE-NAH) • *290 million years ago*

APHTHOROBLATTINA WAS AN ANCIENT cockroach from the Carboniferous period. It looked very similar to the cockroaches today. While some Carboniferous roaches grew to be 3 1/2 inches long, very little about a cockroach's basic shape has changed in almost 300 million years! Ancient roaches probably lived a life similar to today's roaches. Some living roaches are scavengers like the ones living in cities and suburban areas today, and some roaches are fruit eaters like the Madagascar hissing cockroach.

Whatever its diet, the lowly cockroach is one of the most successful creatures on Earth, due to its amazing ability to adapt to changes in its environment.

explorer

aphthoroblattina

TOUGH BUGS

Cockroaches have stubbornly adapted to the many changes in their environment for 300 million years. Some of those changes include the devastating extinction event that marked the end of the Paleo-zoic era and the mass extinction that marked the end of the Cretaceous (krah-TAY-shus) period that wiped out most of the reptilian creatures that ruled the land, sea, and sky, and they have even been able to adapt to the rise of human civilization quite nicely. We humans have devised deadly chemical pesticides to wipe out cockroaches, but the scrappy little insects have managed to not only recover from our chemical attacks but also to become resistant to them. Humans have been forced to design ever more lethal weapons to kill cockroaches, but if the past is any indication, cockroaches will be here long after humans have disappeared from planet Earth.

Mesozoic Arthropods and Their Relatives
—Life Among Giants

IMAGINE: ABOUT 180 MILLION years ago during the Jurassic period, in an area of the world we now call North America, a herd of giant apatosaurs is grazing on the trees they love to eat. Cicadas make an ear-splitting whine that cuts through the hot summer morning, and crickets chirp as they dodge the huge herbivores. Eating is pretty much a full-time job for *Apatosaurus*, so the animals don't even notice the busy little creatures living around and on top of them. Tiny parasites crawl around their pebbly skin and feed on their blood. Hundreds of damselflies, dragonflies, and wasps zip back and forth, preying on the bloodsuckers, picking them off the rough reptile skin.

As they move on to the next grove of trees, the apatosaurs leave something behind—big heaps of dung. As the vibration of the dinosaurs' footsteps fades, small black dung beetles converge on the piles of droppings, roll them into balls (snacking on them in the process), and then roll them away to be buried. As the lucky dung beetles maneuver their treasure across the landscape, others scrabble over to try to steal it away. Tussles over dinosaur dung break out all around the clearing. Eventually, the dung beetles bury the dung, which becomes a secure place for the beetles to lay their eggs and supplies nutrients to the soil.

During the Mesozoic era, insects and other arthropods were all around. They adapted to the rise of the dinosaurs and flourished while other creatures became extinct.

THE ARTHROPODS OF THE MESOZOIC ERA INCLUDE:
Aphodiites (a dung beetle), *Eryon* (an early crustacean), *Icriocarcinus* (a crab), *Archaeolepis* (a moth), *Heptagenia* (a mayfly), and *Protoparevania* (an ancient wasp).

ARCHAEOLEPIS

(ARE-KAY-OH-LEEP-ISS) • *140 million years ago*

ARCHAEOLEPIS IS THE OLDEST MOTH discovered so far. Like moths today, their wings were covered with scales. But unlike today's moths, *Archaeolepis* didn't sip nectar from flowers—it had mandibles (MAN-dih-buls), or mouthparts, made for munching on pollen grains or plant spores. The tubular strawlike tongue that today's moths use to eat with did not evolve until flowers developed. The landscape of the Jurassic period did not include flowers or even grass; these plants did not develop for millions of years.

HEPTAGENIA

(HEP-TAH-JEEN-EE-AH) • *140 million years ago*

HEPTAGENIA IS AN ANCIENT MAYFLY that looks very similar to the mayflies you can see flitting above lakes and rivers in our modern-day world. *Heptagenia*'s back wings were much bigger than those of today's mayflies. Paleontologists believe that *Heptagenia* and other ancient mayflies probably had a similar life cycle to today's mayfly.

Heptagenia was probably prey for other insects, like dragonflies, as well as for the flying reptilian pterosaurs and the fish that lived in the rivers and lakes where *Heptagenia* lived.

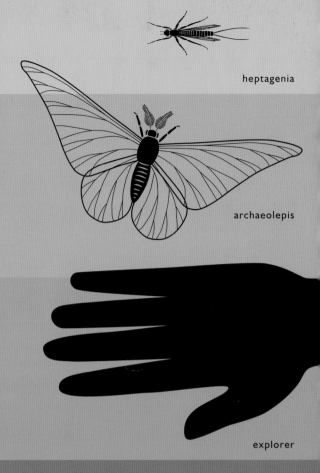

heptagenia

archaeolepis

explorer

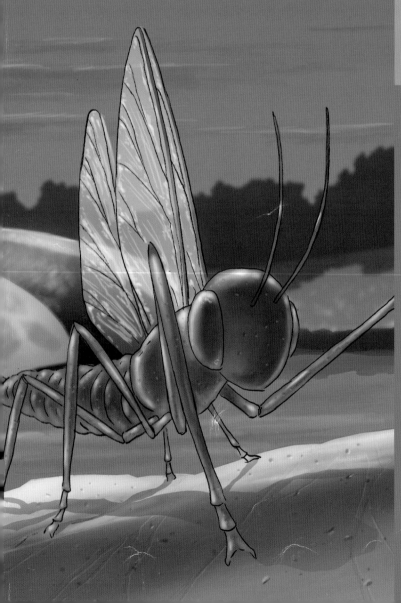

MAYFLY LIFE CYCLE

Mayfly females drop their eggs into freshwater rivers and lakes. When the eggs hatch, the young mayfly nymphs eat plants, like algae, that they find underwater. Once they are ready, they leave the water and molt, or shed, their exoskeleton. They emerge as a subimago (sub-ih-MAH-go), meaning they have wings but have not yet matured. The subimago stage could last as short as an hour, or as long as several days. Then the mayfly molts one last time, into the adult stage. Mayfly adults cannot eat, and live just long enough to mate and lay eggs before they die.

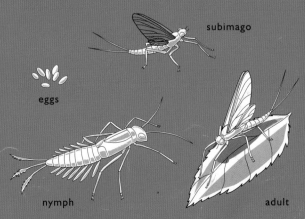

subimago

eggs

nymph

adult

APHODIITES

(AYE-FOE-DYE-IT-EEZ) • *125 million years ago*

APHODIITES WAS AN ANCIENT DUNG BEETLE that first appeared during the Jurassic period. Much of what we know about ancient dung beetles comes from "trace fossils" they left behind in dinosaur dung. In some fossilized dung—called coprolites—there are tracks, tunnels, and nests that paleontologists think were made by ancient dung beetles as they busily cleared the dung from the land. It's likely that today's dung beetles clean up after elephants in much the same way that their ancestors probably cleaned up after dinosaurs.

aphodiites

explorer

TODAY'S DUNG BEETLES

*Dung beetles in the African grasslands and
other places around the world perform an un-
pleasant but very important function. They bury
the huge amounts of dung dropped by elephants,
rhinos, lions, and the scores of other creatures
wandering the plains. If all the animal droppings were left sitting on the ground, they would
attract flies, spread disease, and kill vegetation,
all of which would have a big impact on the
whole environment. The beetles eat the dung
and build nests in it for their eggs. Once the
beetle larvae hatch, they use the dung ball as a
food source (yuck!) until they reach adulthood
and tunnel out.*

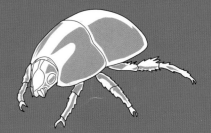

ERYON

(EER-EE-ON) · *180 million years ago*

Eryon was a stout, stubby, ancient lobster. You might not look at it twice if you saw it in a tank at your local supermarket. It had a wide carapace with jagged edges that may have been used for defense. *Eryon* would have used its claws to catch food or defend itself from predators. Male lobsters today use their claws to fight with other males for the right to mate with female lobsters.

ICRIOCARCINUS

(EYE-KREE-OH-KAR-SIN-US) • *140 million years ago*

ICRIOCARCINUS WAS A SMALL CRAB that lived in the Cretaceous period. Like *Eryon*, one front pair of its limbs were claws, which were probably used for defense or for catching and cutting up food. Like today's crabs, *Icriocarcinus* probably lived on the ocean floor, sifting through the mud and sand for prey. Both living and extinct crabs possess a flat tail that folds up under its hard-shelled thorax, unlike the tail of a lobster, which stretches out behind it.

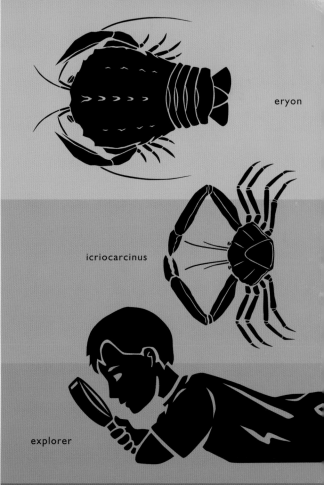

eryon

icriocarcinus

explorer

CRABS AND LOBSTERS TODAY

Crabs and lobsters live in many places around the world. Some prowl the ocean floor for food. Some skitter about on the sandy beach. The largest crab in the world today is the Japanese spider crab, which has legs that span up to 14 feet! Some species of crab are meat eaters, others eat only plants, and some eat both.

Lobsters are territorial, aggressive carnivores that will eat anything they can catch, including other lobsters. If you have ever seen lobsters in your local grocery store, you may have noticed that they usually have rubber bands around their claws. This is because lobsters will attack and eat each other if given the chance.

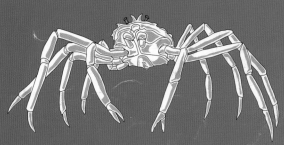

PROTOPAREVANIA

(PRO-TOE-PAH-RAH-VAY-NEE-UH) • *80 million years ago*

THE CRETACEOUS PERIOD WASP *Protoparevania* may have evolved to take advantage of a new food source—not for itself, but for its young. *Protoparevania* may have had a parasitic relationship with insects such as cockroaches, living around them. The wasp may have laid its eggs on the egg cases of the ancient cockroaches, which later served as food for the emerging young.

The wasp itself would have taken advantage of another new food source: flowering plants. Flowering plants made their first appearance during the Cretaceous period. Nectar from flowers would have been high-energy food for *Protoparevania*.

Paleontologists have classified this ancient wasp with certain wasps that we see today, like the modern-day wasps of the family Evaniidae (ee-vun-EYE-ih-day), which also have a parasitic relationship with other insects.

protoparevania

explorer

PARASITIC WASPS

Wasps belonging to the same insect family as Protoparevania are still around today, which shows that the strategy of laying eggs on other insect egg cases is a good way to ensure survival of their own young. Parasitic wasps live alone, instead of in a nest with many other wasps.

Wasps today are parasites on cockroaches, caterpillars, and grubs. Each type of parasitic wasp has a particular insect it hunts for this purpose. One huge wasp—the tarantula hawk wasp—actually hunts down and paralyzes tarantulas (without killing them), which then become hosts for the wasp's young.

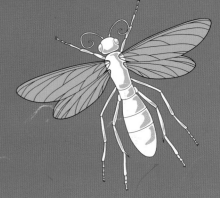

SPHECOMYRMA

(SFEEK-OH-MER-MAH) • *80 million years ago*

ANTS FIRST APPEARED ON EARTH about 100 million years ago. They evolved from non-social wasps, meaning wasps that didn't live with other wasps in a nest. *Sphecomyrma* is an ancient ant that resembles the oldest wasps, as well as the modern-day ants that invade our houses and kitchen cupboards today. At the end of the Cretaceous period when *Sphecomyrma* lived, ants were rare. It wasn't until after the extinction event that wiped out the dinosaurs (except birds), and other giant reptiles, that ants spread all over the planet. Worker *Sphecomyrma* ants have been discovered preserved in amber.

sphecomyrma

TRAPPED IN AMBER

Sometimes, paleontologists find some amazing fossils of ancient insects preserved in amber. Amber is formed when sap from trees becomes fossilized. Tree sap prevents bacteria in the air from attacking the insect trapped inside, protecting it from rotting away. Insects, or anything else, preserved in amber look as though they have been frozen in time. Recently, scientists revealed a remarkable fossil of a spiderweb and some of the spider's prey miraculously preserved in a small chunk of amber.

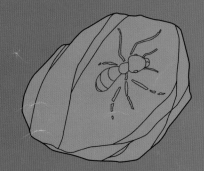

Cenozoic Arthropods and Their Relatives
—Inheriting the Earth

IMAGINE: TWENTY-FIVE million years ago, in the part of the world we now call North America, the hot, hostile landscapes of the Cretaceous period are gone. The world looks very different than it did when the dinosaurs walked the planet. The trees are similar to those we now see around us. There are wide stretches of grassland, with giant mammals grazing contentedly. There are also colorful flowers, which developed midway through the Cretaceous period and have overtaken the more primitive types of plants that had been common during the Mesozoic era.

It is late spring. The sun is warm, and a breeze ruffles through the long grass. A creature like a huge bear, with long curved claws and a face that looks something like a horse, snuffles into view, blinking in the sunlight. This is a chalicothere (KAL-ih-ko-theer)—a large mammal. This strange creature looks fearsome, but it is an herbivore. It is too big for most predators to attack, so it is in no hurry as it ambles along the edge of a forest.

As the chalicothere rears up on its hind legs to reach some tree branches, there is an explosion of color and movement. Little winged insects—the world's first butterflies—emerge from the tree. One of the butterflies alights on the mammal's nose, and uncoils its long tongue to suck up some of the moisture there. The chalicothere shakes its head, dislodging the little insect, and pads off to find a quieter place for lunch.

The butterflies flit off into the warm afternoon, lighting on flowers to sip nectar. They will need energy before starting the next leg of their migration to their summer home. Each butterfly has picked up tiny grains of golden pollen from its visit to the colorful flowers. As they visit other flowers, they will leave the pollen behind, fertilizing the flowers, making it possible for the flowers to reproduce and spread.

The world changed a lot after the devastating extinction event that caused the death of the dinosaurs and other giant reptiles of the Mesozoic era. Mammals and, for a time, giant predatory birds were at the top of the food chain. Insects, like butterflies, and other arthropods increased in number during the Cenozoic era and could be found in almost every habitat on Earth. The ability of insects and other arthropods to adapt to environmental conditions that changed drastically allowed them to flourish and survive into the present day.

PRODRYAS

(PRO-DREE-AS) • *40 million years ago*

PRODRYAS LIVED DURING the Cretaceous period about 40 million years ago in the part of the world we now call North America. Based on fossil evidence, scientists believe that *Prodryas* looked very similar to today's butterflies. In fact, a fossil of *Prodryas* shows what looks like color patterns in its wings. Because color isn't normally preserved, and a butterfly's wings are so delicate, the chances for a fossil of that type to be formed are very small. *Prodryas* looks to have had similar bands of color on its wings as the butterflies we can see in our present-day world, and its coloration would prob-ably have been for similar reasons. Color can help to hide an animal or make it stand out as a warning not to touch it. That amazing fossil of a long-extinct butterfly gives us a glimpse of what the ancient world was like.

prodryas

explorer

NEW WAVE
OF FLOWERING PLANTS

*Like animals, plants also evolve. Some species
became extinct due to climate changes and
extinction events, while others thrived.*

*Flowering plants developed during the
Cretaceous period, and evolved an amazing
symbiotic (sim-bee-OT-ic) relationship (one that
benefits both) with certain insects like wasps,
bees, and butterflies. Insects are attracted to the
flowers by color and scent. The flower provides
the insect with food in the form of nectar. As the
insect feeds on the nectar, it picks up
pollen grains, which are rubbed off
on other flowers the insect visits,
fertilizing the plant so it
can produce seeds.
This strategy has
proven so effective that
insects and plants have used
it for tens of millions of years.*

Arthropods Today

INSECTS AND OTHER ARTHROPODS exist almost everywhere on Earth in amazing numbers. There are far more insects on Earth than people, and more new species continue to be discovered.

Humans have had an uneasy relationship with insects and other arthropods throughout history. Honeybees, ladybugs, and spiders are seen as beneficial because they pollinate flowers or control pests. But other insects, like locusts, cause serious damage to crops when they swarm. Fleas carry diseases, like the bubonic plague, which wiped out about a third of Earth's population in the 1300s. Even today, some mosquitoes spread malaria, which is still a deadly disease in many parts of the world.

Entomologists (scientists who study insects) and other arthropod experts continue to document the lives of these amazing creatures that have outlived humans by hundreds of millions of years. Our understanding of them is important, because although we think of ourselves as ruling Earth, the reality is that we share it with insects and other arthropods. The more we understand them, the better chance we have of forming a symbiotic relationship with our multilegged neighbors. We still have a lot to learn from bugs; after all, they've managed to survive for hundreds of millions of years!

Glossary

ARTHROPOD (ARTH-ROW-POD):
a creature with an exoskeleton, jointed legs, and a segmented body.

BILATERAL SYMMETRY (BYE-LAT-ER-AL SIM-EH-TREE):
when one side of an organism is the mirror image of the other side.

BIRAMOUS (BYE-RAM-US):
the two-part legs of some extinct arthropods had sections used for breathing and walking.

CARNIVOROUS (KAR-NIV-ER-US):
meat-eating.

ELYTRA (EE-LIE-TRAH):
the first pair of wings in beetles that have hardened into tough protective shells for the hinged second pair of wings.

ERA (EER-AH):
a period of time that scientists use to divide Earth's history.

EVOLUTION (EE-VOE-LOO-SHUN):
Evolution is a scientific idea, or theory, that describes how a living thing inherits traits or characteristics from its parents. These changes are passed from parents to offspring through genes, the blueprints contained in every living thing's cells. Genes describe how an animal, or plant, or you should be made.

EXTINCT (EX-TINKT):
describing an organism that has totally died out, with none left living anywhere on Earth.

EXTINCTION EVENT (EX-TINK-SHUN EE-VENT):
a disaster that wipes out many living things over a short period of time.

FOSSIL (FOSS-IL):
a preserved trace, like a bone or footprint, left by an animal that has died.

FOSSIL EVIDENCE (FOSS-IL EV-UH-DUNCE):
information that scientists can interpret from studying fossils.

MOLT (MOHLT):
the process by which an arthropod sheds its old exoskeleton in order to grow.

PREDATOR (PRED-UH-TER):
an organism (animal or plant) that hunts and eats other organisms for food.

PREY (PRAY):
an organism that becomes food for a predator.

RECONSTRUCTION (RE-KON-STRUK-SHUN):
the use of fossil evidence to show what an extinct creature may have been like by making a sculpture or drawing of it.

TELSON (TELL-SON):
the name given the tail segment in some arthropods.

TRILOBITE (TRY-LOH-BITE):
an extinct creature that had three sections (head, body, and tail); living relatives of trilobites include lobsters, scorpions, and insects.

Further Reading

FOR YOUNGER READERS:

INSECTS AND SPIDERS
by Nature Company Discoveries
Time Life Books, 1997
A fun, oversized book with lots of great photos
and illustrations. A great introduction to insects
and spiders.

SPIDERS AND THEIR KIN
by Herbert W. Levi and Lorna R. Levi
illustrated by Nicholas Strekalovsky
Golden Books, 1990
This small field guide–type book is packed with
information about the many types of spiders
throughout the world. Beautiful illustrations show
some of the bizarre adaptations that can be seen in
present-day spiders.

DK POCKETS: INSECTS
by Laurence Mound and Stephen Brooks
Dorling Kindersley, 1995
A pocket-sized book with wonderful photos and
illustrations that breaks down insect types by
habitat.

FOR OLDER READERS AND ADULTS:

TRILOBITE! EYEWITNESS
TO EVOLUTION
by Richard Fortey
Flamingo, an imprint of HarperCollins, 2000
An easy-reading look at these extinct arthropods
that not only contains lots of scientific information
and visuals, but also the author's insights about
the nature of geologic time.

WONDERFUL LIFE:
THE BURGESS SHALE
AND THE NATURE OF HISTORY
by Stephen Jay Gould
W. W. Norton & Company, 1989
The amazing story of the discovery and reinterpre-
tation of the strange fossils from the Burgess Shale
formation, along with descriptions and drawings
of the creatures themselves.

FOSSIL INVERTEBRATES
by Paul D. Taylor and David N. Lewis
Harvard University Press, 2005
Photos and descriptions of the many kinds of
fossil arthropods that have been discovered.

Bibliography

Fortey, Richard.
Fossils: The Key to the Past. 3rd ed.
Washington, D.C.: Smithsonian Institution Press, 2002.

Fortey, Richard.
Trilobite! Eyewitness to Evolution. 2nd ed.
London, Great Britain: Flamingo, 2001.

Gould, Stephen Jay.
Wonderful Life: The Burgess Shale and the Nature of History.
New York: W. W. Norton & Company, Inc., 1989.

Gould, Stephen Jay; Peter Andrews; John Barber; Michael Benton; Marianne Collins;
Christine Janis; Ely Kish; Akio Morishima; J. John Sepkoski, Jr.; Christopher Stringer;
Jean-Paul Tibbles; and Steve Cox.
The Book of Life.
New York: W. W. Norton & Company, Inc., 1993.

Hoyt, Eric.
The Earth Dwellers: Adventures in the Land of Ants.
New York: Simon & Schuster, 1996.

Taylor, Paul D., and David N. Lewis.
Fossil Invertebrates.
Cambridge, MA: Harvard University Press, 2005.

Book design by Tracy Sunrize Johnson.
Typeset in Franklin Gothic, Minion, Times New Roman,
and Humanist 521.
The illustrations in this book were rendered in pencil
with digital color.
Manufactured in China.

Library of Congress Cataloging-in-Publication Data
Bradley, Timothy J.
Paleo bugs : survival of the creepiest / written and illustrated
by Timothy J. Bradley.
p. cm.
ISBN 978-0-8118-6022-2
1. Insects, Fossil. 2. Paleoentomology. I. Title.
QE831.B735 2008
565'.7—dc22
2007018174

10 9 8 7 6 5 4 3 2 1

Chronicle Books LLC
680 Second Street, San Francisco, California 94107

www.chroniclekids.com

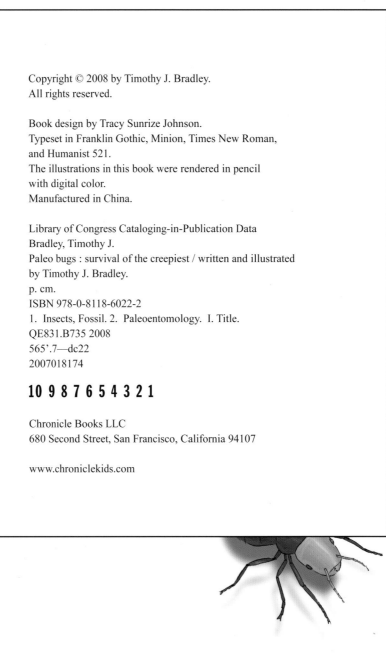